# Reade

"I was invited into this little-k
engaging narrator, and there's a nice blend of dialogue, summary,
scene, and reflection throughout. It's a great reading experience."
—Joelle Fraser, author, *The Territory of Men* and *The Forest House*

"Incredible story, incredible writing, very inspirational. The message:
There is always hope in reaching people who have had difficult lives."
—Liz Shatto, writer

"I couldn't put it down. I love your succinct style that manages to
go straight to the heart ... I truly think you have a winner here."
—Julia Brigden, author, *Girl: An Untethered Life*

"You made an impact on these inmates! Loved the descriptions
of the men. Outstanding writing! Clear and crisp!"
—Margot Grimmer, author, *An American Dance Story*

"I've always loved your story, a compassionate librarian in the
middle of the "tough guy" world, melting the fallen big un-
derdogs with her loving heart, sympathy, and understanding,
yet remaining strong, wise, and witty for them to look up to!"
—Jing Li, author, *The Red Sandals*

"While incarcerated, their life is controlled by strict rules and
locked doors. To maintain any form of privacy, inmates don't
discuss problems openly and keep intimate feelings to themselves. But one day, a new library clerk showed up, Kit Carson,
who was so moved by what she witnessed, that she created this
surprising compilation of stories about incarcerated men and
women, who simply desired a book or a magazine to pass the time."
—Margreet D. Fledderus, Camino blog writer

**Dedicated to all of the inmates (mates) I met
who inspired this writing**

*The Tough Guy Book Club* is a work of nonfiction.
Copyright © 2021, Kit R. Carson

**Disclaimer**
The names and identifying details of the mates have
been changed. These are the general, shared experiences
with books, mates, and library lady in the two Sonoma
County jails.

Published by:
Berkana Publications
Sebastopol CA 95472, USA
Printed in the USA

Kit R. Carson, Library clerk
*The Tough Guy Book Club*/Kit R. Carson

ISBN: 978-1-7354866-1-1

1) Memoir   2) Law and Criminology   3) Creative
Non-Fiction   4) Kindle Short Reads (Memoir)

"Reading without thinking is nothing,
for a book is less important for what it says
than for what it makes you think."

—*The Walking Drum* (1984) by Louis L'Amour

"We read to know we are not alone."
—C. S. Lewis

# The Tough Guy Book Club

A Treasury of Books and People
Behind Bars

## Kit R. Carson

# Table of Contents

## The System:

## Author Notes:

## Thank You:

# The Books

Our library is unique in every way. The books in the main library room are off limits to its readers. Instead, each unit in our detention center has a book cart which is removed, restocked, and returned each week, to the great interest of the inmates. Some have never read for pleasure before. One of the most unique features of our little library is the age of our books—books no one else wants to purchase even for a penny. Our books often come from the remnants of library sales within 100 miles of us, and are the last books left at the end of the day. If we did not take them into our library, they would be dumped into the nearest landfill. You could say that our library was a "literary death row" because the next stop was the county dump—the landfill—death. The 1,000 or so books crammed on pink metal shelves in a room on the second floor of the main jail are old and often out-of-date books, many stamped "Official Discard" on the title page. This is a meaningful metaphor for our readers too, who are the jailed population of our county.

Our library is totally mobile at the Main Adult Detention Facility, although there are small libraries within the units at the North County Detention Facility, (AKA the Honor Farm) where mates are serving light time for less serious crimes. The readers have a touching and meaningful experience with the books, sometimes learning to read.

We have no record of which books are in our libraries, nor how many; no card catalogue nor computer

database, nor any record as to which books are checked out, or by whom, or for how long. Knowledge of the contents of our library rests with the interest and ability of two library clerks, who hope to become familiar with and remember what we have and where it is. We have a system of storage on pink metal shelves where we file and find by sections: Fiction, Mystery, Non-Fiction, Romance, Adventure, Western, Spanish Language, Religion, and Self-Help.

Our books are often outdated in every way, which is particularly noticeable with the non-fiction books, representing countries and political systems which no longer exist, or philosophies and ideas which have come and gone.

We have many best sellers from decades ago. It is, coincidentally, the death row for these books, too—once they are damaged, or show graffiti or gang symbols, they do go straight to the landfill.

Working in the county jail libraries introduced me to hundreds of incarcerated people, who are the clientele of our little library.

Our spare books are boxes of rescued books stored in a small room near the library in the main jail. The

boxes might contain fifty or more books from one person's personal library, since each book in that box would reveal an inscription from years ago when it was given by a family member or friend to the person who had recently died. These books were boxed up and given to county libraries to sell, and in many cases the books were very old—sometimes *spectacularly* old and unique.

But, book by book, connections are made. Some of our readers actually learn to read, others take up reading as a new avocation, some to pass the time, and others using the blank pages in the front and back of books to practice their penmanship and "Old English" alphabets—a style of writing that provided anonymity for the writer who often penned poetic and sad reflections on life and love.

As with any other books, our books provide escape, entertainment, enlightenment, education, and opportunity.

# Honor Farm

The deputies watch us very carefully when we are in the jail modules. It is believed that contraband may most easily be brought into the jail by those of us who are not Sheriff's staff. Before entering the jail, from the lobby of the Main Adult Detention Facility, we are electronically scanned and must wear our special, highly vetted, pass each time we come in. Once inside the main jail (MADF) we must be buzzed, and sometimes escorted by a deputy, into each unit when we deliver a book cart.

I've had nice connections with several deputies and several mates, both up north at the Honor Farm and at the Main Detention Center downtown. It's much more difficult to have any conversation at all at the main jail, because the book carts are simply wheeled in, signed for, and left until the following week. But up north, at the Honor Farm, there are various sized libraries in each of the units, so it's more likely that some conversation and good will can take place by working with the mates in their little unit libraries, or having their help pushing the cart over the cracked, uneven cement path from one unit to another.

In those little moments, here and there, I give them a lot of encouragement, hoping they won't be back.

# Come Along with Me

Our books are already old, many of them out of date, often stamped "Official Discard." For example, books feature names and boundaries of countries that no longer exist as well as philosophies and beliefs that have come and gone.

Yet these books are read, lingered over, and guarded jealously by the mates.

Since the library itself is off limits to the mates, my regular contact with them is in delivering books and reading materials to their units once a week via book carts, each carrying about 300 books. Arrival of the book cart is a big, exciting event. The latest newspapers rest horizontally across the upper shelf of books. Book requests had not been used for years; I brought out the old request forms and encouraged mates to ask for what they wanted, then worked hard to provide for them. In talking with one of the mates about requesting a book, he asked, (speaking of himself) *"But what do I like?"* … it was a place to begin. Another sent book requests with a line drawing of a man behind bars, reading, and he signed his requests "The Tough Guy Book Club."

The job is five days a week and four hours a day. I love providing reading material, answers to book requests, keeping the library orderly, changing books on the carts so they're refreshed and interesting, and opening boxes of other old books for replacements. It's exciting for me to see the mates light up with interest about a book we're discussing. The library serves about 1,000 mates in the main jail, who have been arrested but not yet sentenced, and about 1,000 mates in the North County Detention Center where "light time for light crimes" is being served. I work 50% of my time in the main jail, and 50% at the Honor Farm.

Every day I wake up excited to go to jail. I love my job. The mates are fascinating folks, good hearted for the most part, and very grateful for the service provided through our library.

To come along and meet them with me, turn the pages….

# Six Weeks on the Job

I was out at the Honor Farm today where I've been coming regularly for six weeks, also splitting my time with the main adult detention facility downtown. As Jail Librarian, the mates seem to trust me and are flocking around with all kinds of questions … including how to spell. They already know that I care—how does that get recognized so easily under these conditions? They are anxious to help me move the library cart around on the bumpy sidewalk between the units, and to open the door for me once we arrive. I love that when I discuss books and authors and subjects with them, they get excited and start to ask for particular materials.

My favorite quote from Mother Teresa is, "We cannot do great things, only small things with great love."

# "Dead Man Walking"

I took the book cart on its rounds at the Honor Farm, then returned to the library in the main jail to find two brand new copies of *Dead Man Walking* by Sister Helen Prejean. Each displayed a yellow post-it. One read, "For General Library at North County Detention Facility" and the other said "Kit Carson … For the women of NCDF," indicating the one book was specifically for the only women's unit at the Honor Farm.

The law librarian was nearby, so I asked him, "Do you know who left these here?"

"No, I don't know," he said, distractedly. When I mentioned the title of the book he burst out, "No kidding! I just paid twenty bucks for a copy for my mom to read. Better put those aside for special people."

I opened the "general library" copy and inside the cover, just past the page of reviews, was a handwritten note: "To my brothers and sisters at the Sonoma County jail—Love and prayers—Helen Prejean."

Back at home, I read chapter one, then sat for a while in reflection. Sister Helen Prejean wrote on page eleven: "I am reading people like Gandhi, Alice Walker, Albert Camus, Dorothy Day, and Martin Luther King, and even the way I pray is changing. Before, I had asked God to right the wrongs and comfort the suffering. Now I know—really know—that God entrusts those tasks to us."

# Help in the Library

O h, Ma'am, this is the longest I've ever been in a library without being kicked out!" shouted the mate seated at the table. The two of us sat alone in the small, multipurpose room, also the library, at the Honor Farm.

My helper, today, had been sent over by a correctional officer to give me a hand. Though his pale cheeks were pockmarked, and the ravages of his life showed on his body, his eyes shone. He seemed uncomfortable in his chair—moving it slightly forward and back almost constantly—as though everything would be okay if he could just get it set in the right place. He told me that he had "been around," with several prison terms behind him. "I know the ropes," he said.

"Ask for me again, please," he went on, offering to help me in the future bringing more books into our little library. The library was small and also served as a meeting room, conference room, tutoring area, and the place for GED graduation ceremonies. It was a perfect setting for working with a mate or two nurturing in new books.

Ready to go back to his unit, his whole face lit up in a smile that was genuine, delightful and downright charming, "I'm the laundry guy from the ghetto."

"Great, yes, I will ask for you," I responded enthusiastically, "What's your name?"

"Louie."

The next time I needed help in the library I called unit 201, but Louie had already been released.

The correctional officer sent over two mates, Mackay and Mr. T.

# Mackay and Mr. T.

When I asked for help, an officer in one of the units provided a couple of volunteers to work with me in the library at the Honor Farm. Today, I had two fellows named Mackay and Mr. T., who were escorted to the library, walking stiffly, as if they were errant students entering the principal's office. "Just call me Mac," said Mackay. I discussed the stacks of books and how we would bring them into our collection. After I assigned a classification, one of them would tape the sticker on the lower spine of the book, and the other would apply the self-inking "Jail Library" roller on the page edges then stamp the inside of the first page "Inmate Education Program."

Mac and Mr. T. sat side by side at a long table, Mac behind a stack of books with sheets of stickers (fiction, adventure, western, romance, or non-fiction) plus the old, heavy-based tape dispenser; Mr. T. ready to man the roller, stamp, and inkpad.

We began. For each book, Mac removed a little sticker from the sheet, taped it onto the spine of the book, then pushed the book over to Mr. T., who rolled the page edges first, restacked the books neatly, then methodically opened them one by one. Inside the cover he stamped "Inmate Education Program" officiously, as though he were stamping a WWII exit visa from an occupied country. They could have been in the movie *Casablanca*.

We finished in two hours.

"Hey, guys, pick out a book before you leave," I suggested, knowing that the library itself was technically off limits. "I'll write a pass for you to carry the books back to your unit." Mr. T. said he had never picked out a book in his life and looked worried.

"Take your time," I said, "just look for something you think you might like and give it a try."

"*But what do I like?*" he asked me, earnestly.

"Think about something that made you feel curious or good when you were young—a place to visit you'd never been before? A kind of work you thought you'd like to try when you grew up? Maybe someplace different to live? Cool cars? Take your time and look around, I think you'll find something."

I moved around being busy, so he wouldn't feel any pressure—he may have been asking himself: *Who am I? What do I like?*

Mac had already found an oversized book of photography produced by National Geographic, and was casually turning the pages.

"I GOT IT!" Mr. T. shouted out. I waited to see if he wanted to show it to us, but he kept the book close to his chest. As they were leaving, Mr. T. turned back to face me and said, "Hey, you're alright. You can call me T-Bone."

T-Bone left with an impish grin, still protecting his new read from wandering eyes.

# 201

Unit 201 was scheduled to get their new bookcase today, delivered at eight-thirty a.m., but when I arrived at the Honor Farm at 9:30, it wasn't there.

I called over to the jail industries wood shop. "Just wondering, what's happening with the new bookshelf for 201?"

"Oh, sorry, the delivery just slipped my mind," the instructor said. "I'll have it over there by ten-thirty this morning."

I began sorting through books on one of the two book carts parked in the library, disposing of trashed books—ones with missing pages, a broken binding, or graffiti. With that task out of the way, I filled up the cart with lots of new reading for 201. I was sure the mates would be excited about having so many more choices in their new, expanded bookcase. To top it off, I had come across eight westerns in a storage box I'd opened earlier in the week, so I added those too. Westerns were like gold—more in demand than any other books.

There was plenty to do in the library, so I worked there until around 11 o'clock, heading over to 201 with a cart full of fresh books.

The new bookcase looked great. Over in the wood shop where I had seen it days before, it seemed huge. Now, here in the unit, it looked small. Still, it was two times larger than the old one, this one being about 16" wide and 32" high. The mate in the wood shop who had worked on the 201 bookcase project told me that he was a cabinet maker, and had designed the shelves himself. He was quite proud, and rightly so.

That was yesterday.

Today, as I arrived at 201, there *he* was on the smoking bench outside the door; he had been living in unit 101, one of the larger units with the more trusted mates, but today was demoted to 201, the more restrictive unit—the one nicknamed "the Ghetto." It was the unit he had built the bookcase for.

"Hey, I'm here now," he called out to me as I was arriving. "They 'rolled it up' and sent me over," meaning he had to roll up his sheet and blanket and carry them over to unit 201.

I went inside to bring in the "new" books and he followed, telling me more. He said that some of the guys in the wood shop were stealing the redwood he was using to build bookshelves and benches. "I wrote my name on the bottom of the wood," he explained, "but the foreman said I was defacing property and called it graffiti. So here I am, rolled back to 201." I had heard the foreman's story earlier that day; he said he caught the guy writing his name on the bottom of a bench. Sounded like a misunderstanding. Sadly, there went a great work gig for a nice guy who took pride in his work and really wanted to please.

Inside 201, the mates were shocked that they could take any book they wanted off the cart, stacking them in their new bookcase until the shelves were full. One of the mates started to pick a western off of the cart, and I told him he could put all of them in their bookcase. He was stunned, and moved them quickly. I had custom loaded this cart especially for 201's new bookcase, particularly westerns, and a smattering of the best books I could find in our unusual library of "second chance" books. Before I left, the little bookcase was crammed with choices.

A Black mate approached the cart as I was preparing to leave and put a book in my hand, asking "Do you think this is a good one?" I looked it over. It was one of those novels with sex and mystery, by an author I'd never heard of, and before I gave an opinion, he reminded me, "I was the one who asked for spiritual stuff yesterday."

"Oh," I answered, delighted. "I thought of you this morning when I ran across a book I love and have read many times. It's called *Siddhartha*, a small paperback, and I put it on this cart for you today." We both looked for it and spotted it in the center of the middle shelf, wedged between bigger books. I handed him *Siddhartha* and watched him turn it over to read the short blurb on the back cover. I observed his face, his hands, his posture. He stood perfectly still while he read, slowly, then a smile began and as he turned toward me it was full on.

"Yes," he said, "yes." Then, "Thank you for thinking of me."

"Oh, my pleasure," I said, and smiled back, hoping the pleasure could be heard in my voice.

# A Very Good Day

As I was leaving one of the units, a mate asked, while holding a paperback called *Metaphysical Poets*, "What does metaphysical mean?"

I hesitated in order to think, but being half-Greek I went ahead and said: "*meta* is a Greek word meaning 'above', or 'beyond'." When used in front of the word physical, it would suggest beyond or above the physical existence. Perhaps it would be that part of us which wonders at the meaning of life; reflects on questions such as "why are we here?"

He looked excited and kept the book.

Later, I checked through Google and found that the Metaphysical Poets were a group of poets who intentionally employed highly intellectual language and complex images, with frequent use of paradox. I'm glad I didn't know that earlier, because the opportunity to simply read and enjoy, perhaps discover images and thoughts that he'd never had, was now possible. The book was in his hands, unencumbered by intellectual definition, and he was excited to read it.

A great day for library lady.

# Poems, Please

I want some poems, but don't bring me any of that poetry stuff," whispered one of the mates to me. I barely
heard his request; it was so softly spoken. I was on my
knees going through some of the low bookshelves in the
big unit, 501, where more of the most trusted mates lived.

I looked up and thought, *if he'd ordered a vehicle
from me, he would have asked for a Jeep rather than a
Jaguar.* I suspected that he wanted to understand something, to be comforted, to be transported to another life,
to read into restfulness, peace, to disappear temporarily
from the life he was living. That was the way it seemed
to be for the mates.

As jail librarian, I did have *one* book of poems
about love, lost love, and struggles in intimacy. It was
so much in demand that I had to keep the book in the
library office, and reproduce sections of it to fill the
inmate requests. The mates used it mainly to copy short
love letters for their spouses and girlfriends living on

the outside. They did not trust themselves to be able to express their own love in writing.

One day, the little poetry book was gone! Someone stole *The Pearls of Love!* Did I put it on the book cart temporarily? When something in the jail is taken, you can rarely find it until the mate is moved to another unit or is released. I'd learned early on in the job that if a book was in high demand and went into circulation, it would disappear immediately.

"Charlie's got it in his locker," a mate confessed to me in a hushed voice, walking with me while we pushed the book cart to the next unit. He told me Charlie was charging by the minute for other mates to use it, and they were paying in cigarettes.

It was heartening to know how important a book of simple love poems could be to the guys. Eventually the book was found and returned, and I continued to copy sections of the book to satisfy the many requests. It indeed had been in Charlie's locker. It reminded me of the guy who stole the *Qu'ran*, a beautiful book with gold gilt pages, partly in Arabic, which he took home when he was released. It had the jail ID all over it, but he still took it. He really wanted that inspirational book.

But today's new request—"poems, but don't bring me any of that poetry stuff"—seemed not so much about love poems, but a way to shine light on a life for someone whose life no longer made sense. We had a snippet of conversation in passing; he looked down and I could see his eyes tearing up, and how he blinked his tears away. "Please," he whispered as he made eye contact with me.

As soon as I could, I brought him some writings by Billy Collins, Mary Oliver, and lyrics from a few great songs of the 1960's. I saw him a couple of days later when I was returning to his unit. He gave me a tiny nod and a simple, shy smile.

# Honesty

I rolled the cart into the women's unit and immediately several women grabbed at a book lying across the top shelf of books. It was by Sanford, from the thriller *Prey* series. There was an inmate request slip in it, already spoken for by the mate who had asked for it.

"It belongs to someone else right now, but you can put in your request too," I said.

On my way to the next unit, I noticed that someone had taken that book anyway, and left the request slip on top of the cart.

Back at the library, a Lay Minister was sitting at the table waiting for inmates to show up and remarked, when I told him about the book disappearing. "You didn't expect to find honest people in here, did you?"

"Oh," I responded quickly, "Yes, I've found quite a few honest people here, and a lot of nice ones too."

"Yes, yes, of course," the Lay Minister cleared his throat self-consciously and went on in a lowered voice,

"There are some honest ones," he stammered, his voice drifting off.

I wondered if he had helped anyone in his ministry? *You've got to open your heart,* I found myself thinking, but said nothing more.

# Anonymity

There is a print style used by mates throughout our two county jails that must be learned. It's a three-dimensional-appearing gothic script, using block letters with shaded silhouettes. This script carefully hides the identity of the authors of messages painstakingly scripted in the library books as they circulate through the jails. The mates might print their messages on the opening pages of our books, in the blank spaces after the preface or before the opening paragraph of the story. Or, they may appear in the plain half-pages above the opening lines of new paragraphs or chapters. Sometimes they write in gothic print in the margins, and continue on the blank pages at the end of the last chapter. The script provides perfect anonymity for the poetic, reflective, sad, and sometimes hopeful words that are penned by the mates.

Then again, in normal script, sometimes on the title page, mates briefly review some books for the other mates. Examples of the messages penned are: "This one sucks," "Don't waste your time," "Don't bother with this one" or "One great book." I've also seen "Read this," and once I saw "Best book I ever read." I found this one today: "If I had an hour for every time the author used 'I,' my jail sentence would be served and I'd be out, free."

Recently, a small, thin, pliable book with a handmade dust jacket taped carefully over it appeared. The paper used for the dust jacket had been the cover of an Arthur C. Clarke science fiction book, *Rama II.* The graphic behind the title showed a huge spacecraft with a red EV1 helicopter hovering over it, but inside that careful wrapping was a Spanish language version of the New Testament. The book was perfectly concealed from the judgmental eyes of others.

I wondered, reflectively, who was the reader who so carefully disguised this book? *Where is he now?* And the authors who painstakingly wrote their messages in the margins and blank pages of our books, *where are they?*

# Lunch at the Library

Arriving at the Honor Farm between 9:30 and 10 a.m. gave me time to get things in order before setting out for the modules. The library was on the far corner of the administration building, right by the secure door to the courtyard beyond which the modules were scattered. The library was across the hall from a room of common tables where they chowed down meals in fifteen minutes, then returned to their units. The mates smiled through the library windows as they stood in line to eat; sometimes knocking on the glass to grin and wave. I'm so glad the library was a warm, welcoming place, bringing cheer to mates often facing serious outcomes.

Later, when I was in the library in the main jail, getting books from the storage room, one of the mates working on his case in the law library asked me, "Which modules do you have?"

"I'm strictly at the Honor Farm these days."

"Oh," he exclaimed, "You're the angel from the Farm!"

I nodded and thought, *I'm so glad that I can make a difference.* I was discovering again and again what relief a simple book could bring.

Most of the mates were very appreciative of *any* effort made on their behalf to make their lives one tiny bit easier or more enriched. They are unbelievably grateful and polite, hoping to be helpful and noticed.

Inside an old book, earlier, I saw the words "Jail Sucks." *But, not for me,* I thought.

# The Artist

Today at the Honor Farm, I looked for the artist when I got to 301, the women's unit. I don't know if she's an artist or not, but she has the same name as a world renown artist from the 1900's.

She told me recently that I was the only person who had tried to help her.

"I'll be leaving in four weeks, getting out at 12:01 a.m., and have no place to go except with my ex-boyfriend, who has my van and will pick me up. Do you know where I could go?"

I checked with a friend's daughter later that day— she had been in and out of jail dozens of times.

I asked, "Where can a woman go at 12:01 a.m.?" The daughter, who was a hooker, thought I meant something related to her own profession, but then understood I was simply talking about a woman's release time.

She barked, "She does not have to get out at 12:01 a.m., she could get out at 8:30 a.m. Do I have to go back to the jail and show 'em how it's done?" We both laughed.

I found the artist the next day working in the greenhouse and passed on the information. "Oh, that's what I did last time," she said.

"So," I said, "did you know you don't have to leave here at 12:01 a.m.?"

"Yes," she said, "but my ex keeps saying he'll pick me up and I'll be safe with him."

I urged her to wait until mid-morning to leave jail, and she asked again where she could go at 12:01 a.m. "Ask the officer in your module; say you're getting out shortly and need to find a program to enter. Ask for help."

She thanked me sincerely. "I know it's a good idea to ask other people," she whispered.

"I do it myself," I said, "whenever I'm making really important decisions, I check with good friends first to get feedback." I asked her if she had anybody she could contact, any family, or friends?

"No," she said, "My mother's dead," and started to explain.

"Okay," I said, "your mother is not a possibility. Dad?"

"Very sick."

"Brothers, sisters?"

"No, and no cousins. I have one aunt who is sixty-six and she says she'll come and visit me but she never gets out of the house."

I know I can't fix her problems. I'll do what I can to be fair and authentic. I wish I could do more.

# Meeting Bennie

Bennie is back in 101 again. He had been moved back and forth to 201 for discipline, then 101, 501, back to 201, etc. His book requests, though, were consistent—either WWI or WWII books. After weeks of delivering his requests, I realized he had all of the books from that section of our library spread around only in the modules where he'd been. I asked him to exchange the books with me each week, so I could answer other requests for them and put them back into general circulation. He looked dazed.

He was a medium big man and didn't appear to have any teeth left. He rarely spoke but nodded constantly as if he was drifting. I couldn't get his attention so I tried an imitation of Judge Judy, raising my voice, speaking rapidfire: "Bennielookatmenow,lookatme,makeeyecontactwithme," which he was then able to do. I went on, "Next week, if you are finished with the book I've brought you today, give it to me, and I'll give you another one. Okay?"

He nodded, still looking dazed.

"Bennie, repeat back what I just told you, please," and he was able to do it. He turned away with his new book and as I moved back to the cart I saw one of the officers smiling my way. They like it when we "civilians" can handle the mates. A second smile came my way as I was leaving.

Returning the next week, Bennie hadn't moved units and was still in 101. This time he came right up to the cart holding a book out in front of him like a carrot he was following. He put it right into my hands and I was able to direct him to the top shelf on the other side of the cart, which had fifteen new westerns on it. Bennie's face lit up and he moved into the little crowd with the rest of the mates, trying to get one for himself. And he did. Getting ready to leave, I noticed that *all* of the westerns were gone.

Since this unit was my first stop that day, I needed more books to finish my rounds. One of the mates standing nearby told me where books were stashed—in a closed cupboard between bookshelves in the alcove where four guys were playing cards. I walked over and opened the cupboard and there was the entire collection of new westerns. I said out loud, hoping the right mates would hear, "This is my first stop and I need to take some of these westerns for the rest of the guys in the other units."

One of the card players said "Hey, I can read one of those in a day. I'll be finished with them by the time you come next week … I put 'em there myself."

I asked him, "What if I stopped in 201 first today and let them take all of the westerns? There would be none for you." He didn't respond.

Timing is important. I want my interactions to be caring, instructive, and clear—not punitive, demeaning, or humiliating. This is, after all, a civilian service job under the auspices of the Sheriff Department's Inmate Services Program. For me, the key word is service.

The story's in
our minds...

Are from the
books you leave
behind...

*From 301 to Library Lady*

# 301

Went to 301 first today, the only women's unit at the Honor Farm. It's protected by high fencing with a roll of barbed wire on top for the women's protection in an otherwise all-male facility.

They mobbed the cart as I arrived and, since it was my first stop, I had a full array of magazines on board. "Okay, everyone, just remember this is my first stop and these are all of the magazines I have for everybody today. I'll sort through them so you can see them, then I'll leave about a third of them here." A woman behind me patted me on the shoulder to let me know they understood. She then asked for a *People*, which I gave her, then she saw *Car and Driver* and said, "Aww, how 'cum the guys get those?"

"You can have it if you want it," I said.

"Really, could I have that one?" she said as she reached out for the *Car and Driver*.

"Sure," I said, and kept bringing out more from the bag.

"Oh," she gasped when she saw *Car Craft*, "could I have that one instead?"

"Okay," I said, "Just take one though," and she was jazzed. She patted me briefly on the back again.

After disbursing the magazines and putting the rest back in my canvas bag, I walked back over to the cart, which was surrounded by activity. "Well," I announced with my particular brand of humor and affection, "I'm certainly happy to see so many readers today." They laughed. They've come to understand me pretty well. "Do you know how much we appreciate you?" one of them said next.

"Yeah, really," another woman added. I looked up and many were looking at me.

"Do you know how much I like this job?" I asked. "And, do you know how much I like to see all of you each week?"

"You do?"

"Oh, yes," I said, sincerely. "Every day I look forward to going to jail to see you all and bring the best reading material I can find for you."

"Wow," they gasped. "Wow."

# Where?

I reminded myself that yesterday, a tall, buff man had "traded" me for a brand-new *Ebony*—he was to give me a couple of older ones, but wouldn't be able to produce his part of the trade until today. He said the older *Ebonys* were under the mattress of another guy's bunk.

"I gotta' wait until the guy gets back from kitchen work at the main jail," he said. In the meantime, so it wasn't completely based on trust, he gave me two old *People* magazines, which I passed on five minutes later to someone else in the unit.

I wondered where these things were stored and kept out of circulation. Did everyone have favorite magazines stashed under their mattresses?

There's so often a sense of community, friend to friend, even though jails are temporary holding places. The mates often try to help each other by their actions. It's community.

# Exchanges

Today was especially rewarding. I went to 401 (lock-down), 101, and 501/502. A big stack of inmate requests was piled up in canvas bags on the top shelf of the rolling book cart. Unit 101 was my first stop, and Bennie, the fellow without teeth who I worked hard to instruct on how to "exchange" books with me, gave me two fabulous books today. I never have to ask any more. He's become friends with Steve, the mate I get sea stories for, and I think Steve has put in a good word about me.

Bennie was downright pleasant and managed even to chat a tiny bit. Today, he handed me a McMurtry book, historical fiction, and in a little while returned with a Louis L'Amour western. I gave him several special books to choose from, all about WWI, and had given Steve several sea stories from which to choose. They were both very happy with the selections, and gave back more than I brought, hidden books I could not have gotten without them.

Several other mates were extremely polite and gracious regarding the books I brought and requests answered. One of the mates followed me around the alcoves as I looked through the shelves trying to fill special requests. He showed me secret stashes of books behind cabinet doors, and let me in on all of the prized places where mates hid special books. I was able to collect and answer a number of requests from those sources. Then he offered to push the cart over to 501 with me. The sidewalk between modules is cracked and uneven, and pushing a book cart with bent wheels and 300 books was challenging. The plan was to empty the book cart there, and remove all of their older books. It was part of my system to keep books moving and fresh in each unit.

These mates can be so nice, you wonder how they got into so much trouble? They're genuinely responsive to a kind word and want to please. There's so much I want for them too.

# We All Knew

I spent the morning at the Honor Farm working with a couple of mates, finishing up some work in the library from the day before. Two fellows helped me process a stack of boxes with fresh books for our library.

The guys were so funny, the tales they told … good grief! Their horror stories were painful—tales of violent fathers, run-away moms, empty refrigerators, torn clothes, even sisters or brothers who were shot—and no one in their families *ever* believing in them about anything. They told the stories in a funny way, but we all knew how painful it really was.

"We were volunteered for this job by the Officer, but after today we both want to come back again."

"Yes," I said enthusiastically, "I'll be glad to ask for you both next time."

"We're the laundry guys from 201," they announced proudly.

It's no surprise that kindness and appreciation can bring out the best in a person.

# 101 and 301

I saw Bennie immediately as I was arriving in unit 101 today. He told me he'd been hanging out by the door waiting for the book cart. As soon as we got inside, he seemed to move into the room at a normal pace—which, for him, is lightning-fast—and returned almost immediately with fifteen westerns. This was a collection of new (to us) westerns I had left for 101 in the past several weeks. Westerns were usually quite hard to find. Popular books were stashed under mattresses or in lockers and traded for new magazines, or "rented" out by the minute using cigarettes as cash. Bennie had found them by scouring secret hiding places used to stash favorite books, and he knew I would want to share them with others.

I'm pleased to see that Bennie *did* understand the concept we talked about at our last visit; that if he would return a book to me when I arrived, I would be able to give him another special book each visit. But today, he brought me fifteen westerns, so hard to come by. I thanked him enthusiastically and told him I'd have more books for him next week, as I handed him a large picture book of his favorite subject, WWII.

When I first met Bennie, he seemed unfocused and drifting, never speaking a word. Now he had a job—finding popular hidden books for me so that I could bring him something special each week and pass the hidden books to other mates. Bennie was a changed man.

My next stop that day was 301, the women's unit at the Honor Farm. A young, blonde woman in her twenties, who had been waiting for weeks for a book by Jane Roberts, found it on the bottom shelf of the cart. She was so excited, she waved it in the air, showing it to me two or three times.

Today's 301 Officer (they always rotate) had seemed cool and detached in the past but was now friendly. Before, she never looked up to acknowledge me or the book cart; today I heard her say loudly from her enclosed cubicle, "Ask Kit."

"Ask Kit what?" I called back in a friendly tone. She pointed to an inmate standing at the little open window in front of her protected office.

"What's mag-nan-ius?" the mate asked.

"Mag-nan-imous?" I responded.

"Yeah," she answered, her face blushing light pink; she might have thought she should have known the word.

I winged it with my answer, although I hoped I'd be close. "I believe its big-heartedness, generosity of spirit …."

The Deputy said, half-jokingly, "You mean it doesn't mean just a really big size?" Her answer was very close. She simply forgot the heart part, as so many of us might on our busy days.

# Abba Gail

Abba Gail, our guest speaker, came to spend an hour with the women at the Honor Farm in a Conflict Resolution workshop. Her name spelling is unique, as is her story. It's about her teenage daughter being stabbed to death years ago and how she had to go through anger, grief, fear, and transforming experiences until, finally, she *forgave* the man who murdered her daughter.

This took place in the 90's, before the concept of Restorative Justice. She visited him on death row and became an active member of a group allied for families of victims of violent deaths. She had been speaking all over the U.S. and is a tireless advocate for ending the death penalty.

The three-day workshop was put on by "Friends Outside," a group evolved from the Quaker history of helping incarcerated people. Our local "Friends Outside" office was just to the right of the entrance to the main jail, and the volunteers and I got to know each other as I came and went to my library job, stopping in to pick up books they were donating or to hear news. One day, the CEO of "Friends Outside," in describing their conflict resolution workshop to me, asked if I would like to be one of the volunteer facilitators in the upcoming three-day workshop for women at the Honor Farm. My library hours were flexible, so I said "yes" and went through a brief training.

Our first workshop assignment was to rename ourselves for the duration of the workshop, using a positive adjective starting with the letter of our first name. This took a little time, since it was difficult for many to see themselves with a positive name or image. We coaxed *Eerie Elena* into the name *Elegant Elena*, and we nudged *So-So Shelly* into the positive *Sunny Shelly*. Everyone else kept the names they picked first. We all participated—the facilitators chose names too: *Easy Ed*, *Caring Christine* and *Kool Kit*.

*Sunny Shelly* happened to be sitting in the circle next to Abba Gail for the hour that Abba Gail visited and told the story of her daughter's murder. *Sunny Shelly* listened attentively, and although physical contact is not allowed in jail, shy *Sunny Shelly* touched Abba Gail's arm as she talked about the murder, even rubbing her back once in sympathy, then heading to the bathroom to get Kleenex; we all needed it.

After Abba Gail's story was finished, *Sunny Shelly* asked if she could share part of her own story. She told of a relative who had gotten into a jealous rage, came to her home, and shot her brother and sisters. The irate relative then shot her mother in the arm (but intended to shoot her in the heart), then shot her mom's boyfriend, as well as a neighbor who happened to be visiting. *Sunny Shelly* had been shopping at the market during the brutal melee, and discovered it on her return home. She told her story softly and simply, absorbing Abba Gail's strength. We took a break.

I thought of how many people had said I was overqualified to do the job of detention library clerk. My college degrees, and having been a junior-college instructor in media studies, as well as a traveler, were irrelevant. It was also the lowest paying job in the county educational institution which contracted with the Sheriff's Department to provide library services.

After listening to Abba Gail and *Sunny Shelly*, I understood, deeply, the truth about my job. I used to say: "Everything I have ever done has been useful in this job." And that's still true, but now I simply say, "Is anyone overqualified to be of service? I feel lucky for the chance to try."

I thought about a Ph.D. candidate who, years earlier, stayed in our little community while she wrote her dissertation. Before she left, she gave me this poem she had written:

> Fill my empty hands
> and I will give
> saintly, said I.
>
> Give with empty
> hands
> and they will be
> filled,
> was the reply.

# Hey, Wait!

The mates in 201 were the most desperate for anything that could bring distraction, amusement, or illumination—there was no radio, no TV, and the smallest bookcase of all.

Someone had given me a box of magazines—*Car and Driver, Car Craft,* plus *Road and Track.* I also had some *National Geographics, Audubons,* and a couple of *People* magazines. Once I arrived, the guys were excited and ready to grab at the new magazines.

"Listen now, guys, no one move or touch the magazines until I'm finished putting them out, please." They circled the cart nervously moving and jockeying into position, hands and fingers darting impulsively towards the corners of the magazines they wanted.

"Hey, Wait!" I called out more than once; we were all laughing as they'd jerk their hands back, trying to be patient. "Whoa!" I called out.

When the magazines were laid out evenly over the books on the top shelf of the cart, and they had eyed them all, I called out, "OKAY!" and stepped quickly out of the way. They dove at the cart and within fifteen seconds the magazines were all gone and deals were being made as to who got to be second and third in line to read them.

Some people have questioned if there is any value to providing reading material to people who are incarcerated. I say YES, without hesitation, because I see the value every day.

# Short Takes

Note to librarian:

"I want to thank you for all the help you have given me over the last eight months. Your assistance in acquiring the reading material that I have requested has been most helpful. You have help in making a most difficult situation better. Because of your help I am now able to read, write and spell at a higher level. Needless to say my vocabulary has increased because of you. You opened a door for me that I thought never existed. I never Read Book before until now! Again Thank You for your time and patience in helping me to open my mind to Reading.

I'm sorry I never knew your name."

Overheard from a mate:

*"My baby's grandparents beat him to death ten years ago and I haven't been able to get over it."*

Note to librarian:

*"Can I get a copy of* Last of the Mohicans *by Daniel Day Lewis?"*

Overheard from a mate:

*"I would like to live in a community of artists and terminally ill. The bullshit would stop there!"*

One of the men in the unit that housed men arrested for murder, but not yet sentenced, called out to me as I was leaving, saying:

*"Thank you for the awesome selection. We really appreciate it."*

Overheard from a mate:

*"Just a little kindness will go a lifetime with many of us."*

Overheard from a mate:

*"I don't really understand war, but I can recognize integrity when I see it."*

From a mate in 202:

*"I just want to thank you for being such a great library lady."*

Found in the opening page of a book:

*"Pretty good read. Some sex and violence! Not great, but okay!"*

Handwritten inside the book *Bad Love:*

*The difference between God and a lawyer?*
*God doesn't think he's a lawyer.*

*Difference between a hooker and a lawyer?*
*Hooker stops fucking you after you're dead.*

# Sit with Us

I visited the largest men's unit first as I arrived at the Honor Farm today. Two groups in 101 were watching the Olympics, attentive and quietly gazing with concentration at a big screen in one of the alcoves. The picture was clear and colorful. I asked the men in one of the groups, "Are you inspired by the Olympics?" Their responses were mixed; some enjoyed watching but answered with little enthusiasm. I didn't think they could see themselves as successful athletes.

A large, heavy-set Black mate was sitting just to my right as I knelt down and began to go through the books on the low shelves. He asked me, "Are you watching the Olympics at home?" and I told him, "I don't get Channel 4 and haven't seen any of it."

He jumped out of his seat and invited me to take the empty chair next to it saying, "Hey, join us, ma'am, please sit with us and enjoy yourself. Watch the Olympics with us, please." I was touched by his invitation, although I was working, and it didn't feel prudent for me to sit down on the job.

I told him, "Thank you, but I have to get over to 201; I have a lot of books and magazines for them and they're waiting."

"Please, ma'am, none of us is going anyplace right now, they can wait. Please, sit with us; maybe we can get you a soda or a cup of coffee?"

As I dropped into the empty chair, I told him I had just a couple of minutes to watch the Olympics. He offered me a cup of coffee from the machine, but I declined. Several minutes later, I got up to continue my work.

"Thanks, but I've got to get back to work," I said, smiling at the man for his kindness as I left for 201. He smiled too.

Another good day....

# Library Lady

The Mexicans hang out together in their chosen alcove at the very left front corner of unit 101. That alcove is the closest to the door through which I enter. I often bring the cart to a stop nearby the table where they play cards. Today, the one active reader in the group asked me if I have books in Spanish, again, as they are always in demand. We regularly have very few. Today was different though.

"*Sí, hay mucho,*" I answered. He looked startled and made a dash for the cart. Once there, he found the new Spanish section, now almost fully a third of the top shelf of the cart. We had never before had more than two or three books in Spanish in the whole library. I'd been looking for more books for weeks, and last week had found a small box of them in the county Friends of the Library donation room. In exchange, I left several cookbooks (which were in demand for their book sales) and some early first edition history books that were probably worth money to book collectors.

He found a book he liked, and said, "*Gracias Muchisimo*," waving his "new" book in the air while displaying a big smile on his face. He came right back and got a second one. Again, a winning smile and thank you!

Most of the mates show remarkable gratitude and manners, hoping to be helpful, noticed.

When I got up in the morning, I was tired; I hadn't slept well. I wondered if the falling leaves and rain would stir up my allergies—if I would land in the emergency room of our local hospital again.

Once at work, though, all worries disappeared and I was glad for the place where I could be a useful, caring human being. Outside, I may be just another person, but inside the jail I am "Library Lady," and treat the books—no matter their condition—as gifts to share, and the mates as Very Important People.

# 202 Man

I met a wonderful man in 202 today. A few days ago, he had spoken with me about concerns for his daughter's self-esteem, and I found a book for him on how to present positive images and role models for Black children. When I saw him today, he had the book in his hand and thanked me, smiling.

"You just put the right books in my hands without my even knowing what to ask for," he said.

"I'm sure you had a big part in my getting you the right book." He had described his young daughter to me and how upset she was about her image, looking at white girls and being unhappy with her own hair.

"The book is really showing me how to handle things I had been confused about."

We talk for five or ten minutes, a long time by the standards of what is usual, or even allowed, inside the jail. I could have hugged him easily, if we had been any-place else. It was spiritual for me to listen to this man, to witness him, with all of that love and gratitude and hope glowing around his head.

*Hope is the dream of a waking man*—Aristotle

# My Canvas Bag

I had loaded up the book cart with a few new westerns, Spanish books, and a selection of the latest used books processed from rescued boxes in the storage room at the main jail.

My friend John, who had been a pilot in the Vietnam war, had a large collection of war books. Upon his death, his wife shipped them to me for the jail library—including the book he authored, *Pettibone's Law*. I put some of John's war books on the cart as I was preparing it. It was an especially good day for "new" old books. We also had an unusually large and varied number of magazines—plenty for 101, 501, and 201. The women in unit 301 had specific magazines they liked, *People*, *Cosmopolitan*, or *Jet*. I even had a few of those.

First stop: unit 101. I noticed immediately that the Mexicans had been bumped out of their alcove by some new card players. They had relocated nearby. I had about seven Spanish books on an upper corner of one top shelf, and I let them know about the books, calling out "*libros Españoles aqui.*" Four of them dashed to the cart and picked out books from the new section, and other inmates came around browsing and talking. I noticed the mod worker—an inmate who had been assigned a special job in the module—peeking into my canvas bag, the one with inmate requests and magazines for the day. I lightly chastised him for handling the bag. Soon after, I brought out the selection of magazines that were for 101. A lot of activity followed—guys grabbing the magazines, asking questions, or wanting to chat about reading. A Black mate with dreadlocks asked for a "very smart book."

"Hey, ma'am, I'd like something on calculus or trigonometry."

"I think we have something in that line," I told him, "I'll bring it for you next week." He hung around a while, talking. He was nice. It was an unusual request, and he may have been trying to impress, but I would seriously try to fill his request, no matter what.

Walking around the alcoves looking for damaged books or ones to fill special requests, I opened the cupboard near the card players where all of our new westerns had been hidden the week before. Bennie helped me locate them; I'd taken some for the other units, and left some, assuming I could trade for them the following week. The card players were "on it" though, and all of the westerns were gone. I found them in various places throughout the unit; took some, left some.

By the time I got back to the cart and was ready with a helper to push it over to 201, I noticed my canvas bag was empty of all magazines intended for the rest of the modules. This was the first time in a year that someone had gone into that bag and taken anything. I wanted to handle the issue myself, because I knew that *any* small infraction reported to an officer could cause serious consequences to the offender, if not the whole module. (Months ago, one of the guys pushing the cart for me told me he was bumped down to 201, a disciplinary measure, because his "pants were too tight.")

When I got over to 201, their first questions were "Got any magazines? Got any westerns?" I told them their magazines were in 101 and didn't know who had them, but that I would come to 201 first the following week and leave 201's magazines plus those intended for 101. They were fine waiting a week for twice as many issues. I decided I'd put a typed note on the cart next week, addressed to the 101 mates, letting them know why they had no magazines that day, and that the canvas bag was off limits. "Next time," I planned to say, "I'll report to the officer anyone who handles the bag or its contents." I let them know their regular delivery of magazines would resume a week later.

While I had been looking for westerns in 101 and talking with the man who wanted the calculus book, the Mexicans had picked some books off the cart and were back at their new table, close by. I checked behind them, briefly, for books in the alcove shelves, and noticed one man holding a thick, older book. He was glowing like an angel. He looked up at me as I passed behind his chair. Curious as to what made him so happy, I asked, "Que tiene?" He showed me the book, *Historia de Jesus*, one that had been carefully mended by its previous owner. It was obviously old and cherished, part of the collection of discards I recently acquired from the Petaluma Library, but new to us. Today was the first day that book was on the cart.

"I beleeb in Jesus," he told me in broken English, "and I hab de speerit inside." He told me he had been helped by a minister, and that's how he had gotten the spirit. He stroked the book, opening and closing it as he spoke. Such a smile. So open-hearted. The other three Mexicans at the table were respectful, but distant.

He told me he had two years without alcohol and that he had taken drugs too, which led him into trouble. He talked about his good experience with A.A. and how he had found the A.A. book *Lo Veo Bill*, or *As Bill Sees It*, in our one of the alcoves. His English was limited; we didn't really speak for long but when I was about to leave, the man with spirit talked to me once more. He said "I hab bean watching you por weeks, I see you hab d'speerit too."

I smiled. *I hope so*, I thought.

# Westerns

We drove out to California in a 1938 Ford. My fourth birthday was celebrated at the Continental Divide where our parents bought my six-year-old sister and me western outfits for our new life "out west." Once

settled in Southern California, I wore my western outfit night and day, and never wanted to wear a dress again. Dad took me to some rodeos in Los Angeles, and I couldn't wait to grow up and ride the events—to be a rodeo rider.

In the 1950's we got a television set, which we always forgot to watch. But, on Saturday mornings while everyone slept in, quietly and alone, I watched Hopalong Cassidy, dreaming of a life like that for me. Although a lifelong love of horses unfolded, I did not become a rodeo rider.

Many years later, as library lady of our county jail, it became clear through the requests that the most popular reading subject was westerns—and Louis L'Amour the most in-demand author. His more than 300 stories about frontier justice, adventure, honesty, hard work, and the natural elements of land and weather always showed that *one* person could make a difference. One cowboy with a revolver, a rifle, and a horse could set out freely into the harshness of the wilderness, to endure and survive. The vast landscape, itself, was a leading character in the stories of the settling of the West, whether barren, flooding, windswept, or snow covered. Heroic actions were part of living through every day, and justice was swift—often in shoot-outs, quick-draw duels, or a hanging.

Westerns were sought after with unparalleled passion. Why? The inmates themselves were not able to answer that question. Perhaps it was the simplicity of the western story: the main character, often a loner, rides into a huge, magnificent, uncontrollable God-like environment set against which a great drama of good and bad unfolds. Good wins. It's simple and so well written that the journey is embarked upon by the reader over and over again.

# Unusual Incident Today

I missed the mates over the holidays during our mandatory Christmas vacation. I returned loaded up with "new" books and only had time to go to half of the Honor Farm units, so I picked the mates most desperate for books—the lockdown units.

In the farthest unit they mobbed the cart, anxious for new books, asking about what to read, about magazines, and all of this during a long, polite, well-mannered session. A couple of guys jumped up to help me move the book cart and its load of books over the bumpy threshold of their unit door, across the little exercise yard, and up to the door of the other lockdown unit.

I'd barely rolled the book cart to a stop in the second unit when there was some loud shouting from the other side of the cart and it looked like a mate going down toward the floor, with a couple of more mates involved. Oh no, was it a fight? I'd never seen one in three years. It was a one-armed mate who passed out and went into a seizure. The officer on duty, Deputy Nick, one of my favorites, took control in an impossibly perfect way, politely ordering the mates back to their bunks so he could deal with the emergency. He knelt next to the mate, who was now on the floor seizing, and called into his two-way radio for medics and help. The officers came, and finally the medic, but in the meantime Deputy Nick said reassuring things to the seizing mate, "Take it easy, it will be okay," and kept his hand on his chest to help him. At one point he had to roll the mate over, since he started to bleed from his mouth. He had bitten his tongue and was still seizing.

I asked the guys to move the cart over by the wall nearby and stood out of the way.

I straightened their bookcase and took out the damaged books, adding new books to the shelves.

You could hear a pin drop. The rest of the mates were now on their assigned bunks, in various positions between lying and sitting. Mostly sitting. They looked stunned, as though they had just witnessed a death in the family. I wondered, *are they (like me) imagining what it would be like to die in jail? To have a heart attack or a seizure that would kill them? To die alone, away from family and friends, on the cement floor of a lockdown unit, with all of the guys watching from their bunks?* They were upset. Period.

When the deputy finished with the emergency, they helped the fellow to his bunk.

Deputy Nick got witness reports from me and the mates, then spoke to the guys, "I know you're worried about your friend, but he's sleeping in his bunk, so please stay away from there for now." He then invited me to take the book cart right into the bunkhouse and let them pick out books there.

The guys milled around the cart, quietly handling the books. After a while I said, 'That was really upsetting, wasn't it?" A couple of them answered "yeah"; others looked toward me with questioning eyes.

We talked a bit; our words lingered in the air. I stayed around longer than usual. Just about everybody had something to hold onto, to read, before I left.

# Hanging

Over in unit 202 earlier today, a new young mate came up to me and asked boldly, "Do you have any books on how to hang yourself?"

"Well, no," I said, "but we have some books on spirituality which might give you a path to healing and life so that you don't want to hang yourself."

"Spirituality, huh?" he said, pausing and looking down as though considering it.

I got busy answering a question from another mate, and when I looked up he was gone, already blending into the active crowd swirling around the book cart—talking, asking, looking.... I never saw him again.

# Fiction?

While I was working on the bookcases in unit 101, one of the mates and I talked on a number of subjects: overpopulation, the difference between fiction and science fiction, good biographies: Patti Duke and her mental problems, as well as her performance as the young Helen Keller; Zelda Fitzgerald, F. Scott Fitzgerald, Gandhi and the subject of living consciously.

Later, when I asked the officer for help getting the cart back to the library, that same mate volunteered to put his boots on and push the cart for me. He told me he was getting out soon, and this was his twenty-third incarceration. He knows practically everyone at the Honor Farm, is very friendly and comfortable there.

He wanted to tell me what a person he respected had told him about fiction versus science fiction. That person had said that "fiction is all made up, but that science fiction is possible, although highly improbable."

I said, "I think fiction is based on a combination of imagination and real experience, and was also possible, and sometimes highly improbable too." He looked surprised.

"I never thought of fiction as being based on any kind of reality. What you said really catches my interest. I've discarded fiction as a possibility because it seems so untrue." He asked for another biography, then said, thoughtfully, "Thank you for what you said, I'm going to reconsider my ideas. Could you try to find a fictional story for me about growing up in a small town, or something like that?"

"Absolutely," I answered, "I'll look for something this week and see you next week."

He looked surprised, even pleased. I'll bring him a couple of books, hoping that one of them would be just right for his entry into the world of fiction.

# Hawk

I don't remember exactly when I met Hawk Long Flight, a tall, broad-shouldered, classical Native American. He looked out of place in his standard, jail-issue-faded blue jeans marked with large, opaque, white circles on the back pockets. On top, he wore a white tee and faded blue shirt displaying the large, identifying NCDF symbols of the North County Detention Facility, the Honor Farm.

Hawk Long Flight was a Plains Indian—his stature, color, pride, and dignity were the stuff of legends. How did this magnificent being travel from his tribe to a jail in Northern California?

He started a conversation with me when he came into the library to perform his duties as Inmate Administrative Worker, after telling me he would be released in thirty-eight days.

"What do you think of my writing?" The week before he'd shown me a piece he had written for a class he was taking in the jail, about being in the Vietnam war.

"Oh, it's really good. Great vocabulary!"

"Well, I have two college degrees," he said.

"Great, what do you want to do?"

"I don't know; the Vets ask me that too." We waited through some silence. "I could go back to the work I've always done, security," he offered, looking down. "You know, as a Vietnam veteran it's easy to get security jobs."

"How does it pay?"

"About $7 an hour."

"Well, if you can live on that you have a lot of options," I remarked, encouragingly.

"'Course, being a bodyguard pays $50 an hour; I can make $500 in one day."

"Do you want to do that?" I asked. "On a good day you might lose your life for $500, is that a good price?"

"I've had a full life," he began to explain.

I arched back to look up; he was at least a foot taller than I. "Could you be open to something new?"

"Yeah," he mused, "I guess so. I just don't know what to do." Now he looked directly into my eyes and shifted his stance again. He recounted how much he liked the social services. He told me how he used to send street people to certain folks for help and his experience was respected on both sides of the street.

"I spoke with someone on the phone once who didn't know that I was an Indian. If he'd seen me he would have said, like so many other people do, 'Oh, he's just a stupid, drunk Indian,' but he would have been wrong. I was a smart, drunk Indian." He told me he was going to change everything and not self-medicate any longer.

"I'll try to help you get connected," I offered. I'd never before had any intentional contact with inmates after their release. Hawk was smart, and with his two college degrees and good writing skills, seems motivated to figure out his life. I was aware of how many newly released men and women fell into the chasm between jail and the next step—getting a place to live and a job; trying to get plugged into a life again. I didn't know if I could help, but offered to advocate for him in his meetings with county administrative people on the outside.

"Could you meet up with me Friday morning at the homeless shelter on A Street? I will have information on my upcoming appointments then."

"Sure," I said.

The next week, I wound my way through the traffic to get to A Street, just at the edge of downtown. I parked and went into the yard where homeless folks stood talking, smoking, and passing the time.

"Is Hawk here?" I asked, and one of the men went inside to get him.

When Hawk came out, we chatted a bit, then crossed the street so I could get my day planner and note the upcoming appointment. "When is it, and are you sure you'd like for me to go with you as your advocate?"

"Yes, I'd like you to go along. I've always gone alone, but I could use some help."

"I'll do what I can," I said. I wrote down the appointment. Before I left, I showed him the copy of *Dead Man Walking* I had brought so that he could read Sister Helen Prejean's writing on page eleven: "Before, I had asked God to right the wrongs and comfort the suffering. Now I know—really know—that God entrusts those tasks to us." I hoped it would encourage him toward helping others as he had done in the past, rather than being a bodyguard to a rich drug dealer, as he had also done in the past.

Four days later, I picked him up at the shelter on A Street and we headed for the County Administrative offices. The appointment was disappointing. There was an obvious disconnect between the interviewer and us. The questions the clerk asked were rattled off disinterestedly from stapled-together papers and he even snuck frequent glances at the clock while asking them. He was impersonal and distracted. Hawk tried to stay interested, but finally just pulled back and began to answer the questions automatically, carelessly.

After that meeting, Hawk said he was tired and wanted to quit for the day. "I was helping a friend move his mattress and I hurt my back. I've had to take some more pain medication," he commented. "Maybe we can try again next week. Stop by and we'll talk about it."

Back at the shelter I said, "Take it easy," as he crossed the street and headed for his older, small pickup with an oversized camper lodged on top. While starting my car, I saw him trying to fold his tall body down so that he could squeeze into the little front seat of the pickup from the passenger side. It was parked by a telephone pole, and he was having difficulty. The cab looked full of stuff, cluttered with papers and plastic objects. The body of the camper had a horizontal gash in it, with insulation pushing out.

It seemed he was planning to sit in the front seat for a while, like one sits in his living room on a Sunday morning. It was, after all, home.

# Ron Is In

While I was working in the library at the Honor Farm today, a fellow walked by and tapped on the window, smiling enthusiastically. I was sure I knew him, but didn't remember where or why, except that he was a mate. He was coming into the Administration Building and stood waiting for a long time at the door. I left the library and approached the door from the inside, pressing the buzzer. The door opened immediately, and we chatted for a minute as he came in from the secure area of housing units.

"Where are you going?"

"I'm going to work in Admin, going to go around and clean up and empty waste baskets."

"Isn't that Hawk's job?" I asked.

"Yeah," he said, "he's gone. A couple of days ago he walked up to me and said, 'I've been watching you and I think you could do the Admin work,' and I said 'Yeah, I sure could,' and Hawk picked me as his replacement."

"Great. I just left a note for Mrs. Carlyle that trash is on the floor in the library; the waste baskets are over-flowing. Must have happened yesterday afternoon when a large group met here. Could you give me a hand?"

"Oh, sure," he said, "I'll be right back in about ten minutes, take care of it for you." As he was leaving, I discovered his name was Ron because he asked whether I had gotten the book for him. This is a question I am asked a lot, but which book?

"The *Prey* books, Sandford," he answered, excitedly.

"Oh, you're the one. Remember the *Prey* book with no cover I mentioned, the one that needed repair? Well, I repaired it this morning and set it aside but haven't put your request slip in it yet." I told him he could take it with him when he returned because I wasn't going around to the modules today, just working in the library.

When he came back to clean up the mess, I showed him the repaired book. It was *Mind Prey*, which made him very happy.

I asked, "Do I have a request slip from you?" and he assured me that I did. I looked for it again, while he was cleaning, but couldn't find it.

"Maybe you've already put a book aside for me—you said you had a substitute in case no *Prey* books appeared."

"Oh, good idea, let me look," I said, and found a brand-new paperback *Prey* book that I'd traded for the Sonoma County Friends of the Library last week. His request slip was in it. He looked at the new book and said "I can't believe it! This is the one I wanted more than anything."

"Well, it's yours," I said, handing it to him. It was a small paperback, not oversized like the repaired *Prey* book. He assured me he could walk to his unit with it as long as his request slip was in it. Ron was happy when he finished cleaning up and left with the book in his back pocket.

I had a lot of special request books for people that day and decided to make a separate run just to deliver them. I encouraged mates to fill out requests, to ask for what they want, and then I tried like mad to get it for them.

God is in the details.

# Jailhouse Book Reviews

The Ross MacDonald book, *Black Money*, sits on top of a small stack of books in 101. On the book cover is a quote from the *New York Times*, "The finest series of detective novels ever written by an American." Then, inside, "This is excellent book," and, "O.K., slow at times 3 handcuffs out of 5," and another, "If you like mysterys you will like this book. Good Book."

Excelent reading it wisks you away from your cell Top Notch. *read* JAIL HOUSE REVIEW

## Praise for SHADOWS IN BRONZE and SILVER PIGS

"It is everything: mystery, pace, wit, fascinating scholarship, and above all, two protagonists for whom, by the end, I feel genuine affection, and want to meet again."

ELLIS PETERS

SONOMA COUNTY DETENTION DIVISION
**INMATE REQUEST FORM**

| 1. Inmate Name *(Enter full name)* | | | 2. D.O.B. | 3. Housing Unit | 4. Booking # |
|---|---|---|---|---|---|
| Last | First | M.I. | | | |

5. PLEASE SEND THIS REQUEST TO THE FOLLOWING OFFICER/DEPARTMENT:

☐ Program Officer  ☐ District Attorney  ☐ Probation

☐ Public Defender  ☐ Mental Health  ☒ Other *LIBRARIAN*

☐ Friend's Outside  ☐ Classification

6. NAME OF INDIVIDUAL TO CONTACT. _____

7. I WOULD LIKE TO DISCUSS A COMPLAINT. ☐ *(Explain in Comments/Request section below)*

8. I WOULD LIKE INFORMATION. ☒ *(Print in Comments/Request section below)*

COMMENTS/REQUEST: *I WOULD LIKE TO READ AN ENTIRE SET OF ENCYCOPEDIAS, PREFERABLY BRITTANICA, IN CHRONOLOGICAL ORDER PLEASE. IF THAT IS ACCESIBLE, COULD YOU PLEASE BRING ME VOLUME 1, WITH THE SUCCESIVE VOLUMES FOLLOWING AT ONE-WEEK INTERVALS. THANK YOU VERY MUCH FOR YOUR EFFORT.*

9. INMATE SIGNATURE: _____ DATE: *3-25-03*

10. RECEIVING STAFF SIGNATURE: _____ DATE: *3 25-0 3*

# Jailhouse Book Reviews

**INMATE REQUEST FORM**

| 1. Inmate Name *(Enter full name)* | | 2. D.O.B. | 3. Housing Unit | 4. Booking # |
|---|---|---|---|---|
| Last | First | M.I. | | |

5. PLEASE SEND THIS REQUEST TO THE FOLLOWING OFFICER/DEPARTMENT:

- [ ] Program Officer
- [ ] Public Defender
- [ ] Medical Staff
- [ ] Friend's Outside
- [ ] District Attorney
- [ ] Mental Health
- [ ] Classification
- [ ] Probation
- [X] Other **LIBRARIAN**

6. NAME OF INDIVIDUAL TO CONTACT.

7. I WOULD LIKE TO DISCUSS A COMPLAINT. [ ] *(Explain in Comments/Request section below)*

8. I WOULD LIKE INFORMATION. [ ] *(Print in Comments/Request section below)*

COMMENTS/REQUEST:  I WANT TO THANK YOU FOR ALL THE HELP YOU HAVE GIVEN ME OVER The Last 8 moNThs. your ASsisTaNce IN ACquirINg The Reading material That I Requested About has been Most helpFul. you have help iN makiNg Amost diFFicuLt SiTuation beTTer. Because of your help I am NoW able To Read, write aNd Spell at A higher LeveL. Need Less To Say my vocabulary has InCreased because of you you opened a door For me That I Thought Never EXisted. I Never Read Books before uNTiL NoW! AgaiN ThaNk you For your Time aNd Patiene in helping me To open my mind To Reading. I'm sorry I Never Knew your Name

9. INMATE SIGNATURE: _____  DATE: 9-5-01

10. RECEIVING STAFF SIGNATURE: _____  DATE: 9-5-01

# Hope for the Holidays

It was Friday, December 15th, and the nine mates looked excited, wiggly and self-conscious, as they stood awkwardly in blue gowns usually reserved for GED graduation.

Grouped in the center of a big stage, they faced the largest auditorium in the Santa Rosa Veterans Building, with the standard arrangement of chairs for 1,000 people. There were only fifty of us scattered around the room in clusters of three and four, mostly women and children, sitting among rows of empty chairs. The nine mates had been practicing for weeks for this singing performance for friends and families, "Hope for the Holidays." They fidgeted with their gowns, giggled, and made faces at each other as they prepared to sing. Deputies kept a low profile, either backstage or off to the side. The Sheriff's bus was behind the auditorium, out of sight.

Nervous and excited, sometimes singing off key, the mates managed to belt out their entire set of holiday numbers while children ran wild throughout the hall, chasing each other up and down the long aisles, screaming with glee.

After the performance, every child was invited to visit Santa in the back of the auditorium to receive a special gift. The mates in the carpentry training shop had worked for months making these exquisite, old-fashioned wooden toys in the shapes of cars, trucks, and trains, with solid moving wheels.

It may have looked appallingly chaotic to a passerby, but in all of that noise we were having our happy, holiday event.

Tonight, that broken bookcase in the lockdown unit doesn't seem so important.

# Day Services

This Friday, around one-thirty after work, I drove by the Day Services for the Homeless house to drop off a note. Hawk had been released and contacted me at the jail. I watched my note to Hawk get folded and pinned neatly, under "H" on the private, organized message board. It's a large display board just behind one of the administrative desks to the right of the front door and is loaded with a series of little pink folded-up messages, alphabetized and stuck with push pins under the letter of a first name. It is the neatest, most orderly thing in the place. Once my message was pinned up, I thanked the fellow and turned to go.

While leaving, I passed by a young man on the porch who was smoking; he smiled at me and stuttered, "D-D-D-Do you still w-w-w-work there?" I looked at him, not sure if I knew him or not. He added, "Y-Y-Y-Y-You're the l-l-l-librarian, aren't you?"

"Yes, in fact I'm coming from work right now." I asked him about how things were going and he answered "Good"; he had just gotten a job. He told me his girlfriend was in jail right now, in "E" mod in the main jail.

"You guys stay outta' there!" I said, smiling, but with firm intention. He grinned. "Yeah, I know."

It was pouring rain and bitterly cold while we stood on the steps of the porch, "The transition is really hard, isn't it?" I asked.

"Yeah," he said, "it sure is hard, especially in weather like this." By then he wasn't stuttering any more. We stood quietly a bit longer; he seemed glad to see someone he knew.

"Well, you take care and good luck to you," I said, as I reached out my hand to him. He quickly transferred the cigarette to his other hand and shook my hand firmly.

"Okay, see ya," we said quietly at the same time, smiling.

# Graduation

Open House was this week at the Honor Farm. I had a long conversation with the General Education Development (GED) instructor. She, too, loved her work and was very good at it. I went to the GED graduation a month ago and was impressed by the compassionate, proud, personal tone in her voice as she handed out each diploma. The mates stood tall, yet wore an aura of humility.

Graduation was held in the library, with the mates dressed in blue graduation gowns on loan from our local high school. They wore a cap/mortar board too, and had photos taken holding their diploma, standing in front of a tall, full bookshelf.

No one would know that the graduation took place in a jail.

# Unit A

My assignment in the Main Adult Detention Facility included half of the incarceration units in that facility. The units were identified by letters of the alphabet, and I was given a list to visit, regularly, with books. I didn't know who was in the units or what their crimes had been. No one talked about that, and it was neither useful nor appropriate to ask.

In one particular unit, the men were consistently exuberant when I arrived with books and magazines. They tended to crowd around the book cart and mob me with questions and greetings. The deputy in charge watched carefully and made sure they were as mannerly as possible. I was just 5'1" and the men were much taller—the deputy said he couldn't always see me in the little crowd around the book cart. He was concerned. I loved the enthusiasm of Unit A, my first stop in the main jail, where the most passionate collection of men were, and I really enjoyed bringing reading to them. They were grateful that I had taken care to line up books on relationships, healing, and spiritual matters on the top rows of the cart. The books on the other shelves were a scattering of everything else available. The mates thanked me over and over again for the care I took in placing healing materials up top.

One day, in the hallway by the main jail library, a deputy offered to get me a mate to help carry the boxes of books from the storage room just behind the library, and to help processing them with stamps and stickers identifying them as jail materials. I'd never had a helper at the main jail before.

She said, "I can get you a murderer." I thought, whaaaat?

"Oh, that's okay," I said, calmly.

"But they're the safest guys in the whole jail," she went on. "They're not career criminals, they just got pushed to the edge somehow and tipped over!"

The room where we would be working was windowless, and off the main hallway behind the library. We couldn't be easily seen. I had reservations about it, so declined.

After working at the main jail for over a year, the law librarian happened to mention that Unit A was occupied by men arrested for murder. "Really?" I said, shocked, because that was the unit of men so keen on healing, the friendliest bunch of mates at the main jail.

They had been arrested for murder? I remembered that when I first started on the job, the deputy in Unit A was very concerned that I wore a neck scarf, wondering about my safety. "Oh, I've worn a neck kerchief since I first went out into the world," I answered, simply. His brows knit slightly and he raised his shoulders briefly as if to say "whatever."

I would have accepted the deputy's offer to "get me a murderer" if I'd known he'd be coming from Unit A—I'd been serving them for a year already and loved going there.

# Could I Stay?

As I passed through the Honor Farm's security checkpoint, I heard heartfelt sobs coming from the large lobby beyond the front desk. I looked up and saw a young woman, perhaps in her twenties, sitting hunched over in a metal folding chair, holding her face close to her knees as she cried and rocked. I had never seen her before, and wondered why she was there? A large, clear plastic bag was wedged between her feet and she was dressed in street clothes.

Two Sheriff's deputies walked briskly by, ignoring her. Another deputy, whose kind nature I had previously witnessed, approached her as he entered the room, asking softly,

"What's the matter, young lady?"

She looked up at him, unable to catch her breath. I was passing by on my way to the library, and she said, looking up at both of us, "It's so hard to leave here. If we had a swimming pool, I'd stay here forever."

Her remark reminded me of little Frankie in Carson McCullers' book *The Member of the Wedding* when she was described this way: "She belonged to no club and was a member of nothing in the world."

Frankie reflected about herself, "The trouble with me is that for a long time I have just been an *I* person. All people belong to a *We* except me. Not to belong to a *We* makes you too lonesome."

The new minister of a local church described to me her visit to a parishioner who was turning ninety-five and no longer traveled to church on Sundays. "To what do you attribute your long life?" the pastor asked.

"*Community*," the woman answered without hesitation.

# Gone

When I roll the book cart into the units and notice that one of the mates I've gotten to know is gone—either released or sentenced to a prison somewhere else (I never know), I feel a loss. Sometimes I'll have a book or a magazine which I found for them after looking exhaustively, and when I arrive in the unit to deliver it, the mate's gone. I encourage them to ask for what they want, to experience the reward of receiving it.

I happened to see one of the gang guys in the process of being released. He was sitting in the lobby on a Saturday morning just as I was leaving, and we had a brief conversation—a nice talk. He was waiting for his ride home, sitting stiffly on the bench, head down, and looking a bit lost.

I remember it took weeks for him to ask for a book; finally, he did.

Little moments, big memories.

# Conflict Resolution Workshop

Yesterday we started day one of a three-day workshop developed originally by the Quaker Friends, who were committed to visiting and helping people in jails. I have been invited to join in as one of the facilitators and have been given a brief training.

Our workshop consists of twenty-nine women from the Honor Farm, and three facilitators: Ed, who has been leading workshops for Friends Outside for three years; Christine, a kind woman with whom I took the training; and me, who was also the library lady.

Many of the women said they chose to do the workshop because they would get a day off their sentence for participating. Some said they signed up because they were bored. No one said they wanted to learn about conflict resolution.

They wanted to maintain their "tough-guy" face in front of the others, even when our first challenge was to do the "adjective name game," where we chose a positive adjective to put in front of our name. The adjective was to start with the same letter as our first names and was how we would be known for the next three days. Some chose tough names instead of positive ones, which *Easy Ed* allowed for starters, but one brave and memorable woman—big and stocky with a strong presence—chose *Dainty Dottie*. Soon, though, she changes it to *Dangerous Dot*. Other women change to a less vulnerable name too, but since the games are personal and often fun, no one is able to stay completely, emotionally outside.

We spent much of the second day brainstorming violent behavior—what leads up to it, what it is, and what some non-violent alternatives are. Later in the day, as the group was preparing to do some of its hardest work, *Easy Ed*, our senior workshop facilitator, asked the women to describe some violent situations they had experienced. They came up with eight stories, to which they assigned descriptive titles, and voted on the most popular three stories to rewrite and enact for the rest of us. Their stories ran the gamut from "Shopping Day," to "Pool Game," "Neighborhood," "Killer Hair Dryer," "Broken Window," "Child Abuse," "Psycho Cousin," and "Goodbye Dear (Deer)." The ones which the group chose to re-enact, for which they would create non-violent endings, were: "Neighborhood," "Goodbye Dear (Deer)," and "Killer Hair Dryer."

"Neighborhood" involved a six-year-old boy bullying a four-year-old at school and taking his lunch money. The younger boy told his mom about it when he got home, and mom marched over to the bully's house, dragging along both her four- and six-year-olds. She confronted the bully's mother, telling her, "Okay, I've brought my six-year-old, why doesn't your son fight someone his own age instead of bullying a four year old?" The six-year-old boys fought, and the mothers fought each other too.

"Goodbye Dear (Deer)" described a man and a woman in a relationship having an argument. She wanted him to leave, but he had been drinking and wouldn't. Taking a pair of five-point antlers off the wall she "coaxed" him into leaving and called the police. When they arrived he was nowhere in sight, so they arrested her and took *her* to jail.

"Killer Hair Dryer" was about a husband and wife arguing. She was afraid he was going to harm her, so she swung her hair dryer at him, clipping him on the back of the head. Next stop: Emergency Room.

On our final day, we reviewed the stories from the day before; then *Easy Ed* went outside with one group at a time to coach them into rewriting their story endings and rehearsing their performance for the rest of us to watch.

*Caring Christine* and I were left waiting with the twenty-three other mates while the teams rehearsed. I asked, "Hey, would you like to sing while we wait for the performance?"

One confident young woman stepped up immediately, launching into "Somebody to Lean On" with everybody singing the words they knew and coming in loud on the chorus. It was so much fun they decided to do "Reach Out," and had just sung the first line when Ed and the "actors" appeared.

The first team performed "Neighborhood" with a new ending. We sang again until the next group was ready; in fact, we sang through *all* of the breaks and, for the first time, I saw *everybody* participate at the same time, including a Hispanic woman who had kept to herself and hadn't taken any risks.

We facilitators all went to lunch together and used the time to sign Affirmation cards along with a personal note for each mate. During lunch, *Easy Ed* said he had never heard any groups sing before and was sorry he'd missed it. Later, as we were winding down the workshop, I asked the women if they would please sing for *Easy Ed*? Instantly, *Joyful Julie* jumped up and led "Lean on Me." The excitement built and they wanted to keep going, so *Dangerous Dot* volunteered to lead the next one, but she announced loudly, "I am not going to dance!"

We had just found out the day before, in an exercise called "Something about me you didn't know," that she made her living as a pole dancer. By the time she started leading us in "Reach Out," she got swept away, easing snake-like out of her chair, and in a gradual transformation, began her pole-dancing moves. It was wonderful and sexy! Everyone grinned and sang louder, ending with bold, spontaneous clapping.

Later, when we told them they were going to graduate, *Dangerous Dot* was the first one to cry. We let them know that they would be getting certificates too; then one woman after another said tearfully that she has never graduated from anything, had never completed anything.

After the break, we got ready to hand out the Certificates of Completion, along with each person's Affirmation Card. We had our last circle and passed the talking stick from person to person. On my turn, I recalled that Mother Teresa said she saw God in the disguise of distress. Many women, when they spoke, cried and couldn't believe that twenty-nine women could get along in one room, and share such intimate experiences together.

As graduation time arrived, one of the women started to hum "Pomp and Circumstance" and continued as each person stepped forward to get her Certificate of Completion, Affirmation card, and hugs. They hummed the loudest when *Dangerous Dot* stepped up to receive her papers. When it was all over, *Easy Ed* told them, "We are finished."

No one left the room. They just stayed, and one woman shouted out, "Look, we don't even want to leave!"

A few minutes later, Sister Martha (a Catholic nun) came into the room and told us she has just passed a woman crying in the hall who said the workshop was the first thing she had ever finished in her life.

God Bless Us All.

# Meeting Marc

I met Marc in a morning twelve-step recovery meeting. I had been sharing about a young woman I met while jail librarian who described a horrific, personal tragedy, and she still couldn't get over it. I said what a special service it was just to be there, to care, and to bring what I could to the situation. And, I really missed the mates in our local detention centers.

Marc spoke next, said he was just passing through our town and hadn't planned to share, but when I mentioned jail and service, he wanted to speak. "I'm an ex-con with seventeen years prison time behind me, and I'm now recognized as a homeless veteran rather than an ex-con." He said doing service for young men returning from Iraq and Afghanistan is his mission now, to get them off the drink and into a sober, new life. "I'm committed to this," he said. "I'm dedicated and sober."

After the meeting, I offered him some money—ten dollars was all I had—and I asked him to get a good meal for himself. He thanked me and said he was on his way to Guerneville to the Veteran's Hall, where they would also give him some money. After that, he was heading south where he had business to attend.

We hugged. It was special.

He told me about an officer at Leavenworth Prison who came by his locked cell and said, "I know you're different—not a psychopath or a sociopath—and that you really don't belong here." He felt that God had sent that message to him so he could have hope and know that he could be seen by others as a decent person.

We hugged again. As I left, I dashed to a nearby grocery store and bought him a breakfast croissant, but when I returned five minutes later, he was already gone.

# Oh, No!

Hi, I'm Kevin," said the young man to whom I had just been introduced, "and I just got out of jail."

"Oh," I said, surprised because it came out so early in the conversation. "Where were you?"

"At the Honor Farm up north," he answered without hesitation or shame.

"For gosh sakes," I said with enthusiasm, "I used to be the library lady there and it was one of my favorite jobs."

"You might want to know that all of the books are gone."

"GONE?"

"Yeah, all gone."

He recounted that there were issues about the center pages of some books being cut out to pass cigarette stubs from one unit to the lockdown units using the book cart as the transfer vehicle.

I recalled that every once in a while, as I was arriving in a unit, a deputy would remove all of the books from the cart and check every one for evidence of contraband. If no evidence was found, the books would be restacked on the cart, and the day would go on. Once, a stub of a cigarette was found, squished into a small, cutout hole in the center of a hardbound book. The cart was headed for a non-smoking lockdown unit. That book was removed from the cart, and I continued my service. That's all I know.

But to remove all of the books from the jail? Catastrophe!

A year later, I learned that only the hardbound books had been removed, and the paperbacks kept. Talk was that the hard covers could be cut and made into weapons. I felt sad that our odd collection of second-hand books, featuring out-of-date original stories and history, might never be read again.

# The System

# A Little About the System

I know very little about the system, although I worked within it. My assignment was to bring reading materials to those incarcerated in both of the two county jails in Sonoma County.

The Main Adult Detention Facility (MADF) and the North County Detention Center (NCDF, also known as the Honor Farm), are the county jails. At the main jail, people arrested are detained until their trial. At the Honor Farm, mates have already been sentenced and will serve short times—usually a year or less—for "light crimes." Those housed in the main jail remain until judged, after which a guilty verdict could result in being sent to a State or Federal prison for a number of years, up to a lifetime.

A three-year study found that alcohol and illegal drugs were involved in the imprisonment of four out of five inmates in the nation's prisons and jails. And alcohol, more than any illegal drug, was found to be closely associated with violent crimes.

The American Medical Association (AMA) declared that alcoholism was an illness in 1956.

The mates incarcerated everywhere have made mistakes and are paying the penalty. Who hasn't made mistakes, especially life-changing ones?

My job is not to judge, but to serve.

I have written to share my many experiences with the mates during my three-and-a-half years as library lady.

# Who Are They?

While I was in the job as jail librarian, people outside would often ask me to describe the mates, sometimes asking, "What do they look like?"

"They look like you and me," I answered easily. "They're mothers and fathers, sisters and brothers, nieces and nephews, neighbors, and more. Anytime you're in a crowded event, a long line, or a busy supermarket—look around and you'll see them. Their feelings, of course, are like ours with ups and downs, hopes and dreams, successes and disappointments. And there are people with mental health problems, too. But they've made mistakes and been caught at them, unlike many of us."

A number of them are paying with incarceration, a high price for some of the misdeeds. I never knew, nor asked, what brought the mates into jail, my business was to serve, not judge.

# What's at the Heart of It All?

Service, caring, was at the heart of my job … service to the often forgotten, the judged. The mates I met may never have crossed my path otherwise, but I was privileged to witness and experience special insights, passionate change, openness to new ideas and unexpected exchanges.

One of the main difficulties was the constant movement of the mates: they might be released, sent to prison, in meetings, in court, or in motion for some reason.

There was definitely a sense of connection, community, that existed, but sometimes only for a day.

# Author Notes

# Not About Me

When I was at the Honor Farm briefly, before setting out to pick up magazines from Sonoma County Office of Education, a couple of mates talked with concern to me through the open library window.

"Are you okay?" one asked, eyebrows pushed tight with concern.

"Yes, thanks," I answered, "I was on a trip back East to visit family."

"Oh," he said, "we were waiting for you, then we started to worry."

Next day when I started my rounds, I heard several comments expressing concern about me, rather than frustration about where the book cart was. I was surprised at the genuine concern that was shown. I was touched.

There is some writing in this book depicting incidents and conversations that seem complimentary to me, but I honestly believe it's not about me. It's about them. It's about all of us. How do we treat our fellow human beings, and how much does that have to do with how they behave? A little kindness goes a long, long way in life.

# Change Jobs?

A friend just finished training for a job that will pay $30 an hour. It's tech support for an internet-based program akin to the Peace Corps. She said she could easily get me a job. I'd train for a couple of weeks in Berkeley, then work at home from my computer. The money tempted me; I'm making less than $10 an hour right now. Still, I wondered, would I be able to say "I love my job" at the end of the day? Wouldn't I miss the eye-to-eye contact with the mates, who are very interesting folks, and the contributions I could make in connecting reading materials to them while they do their time? Yes, I would miss it all … money has never been more important to me than experiences, and I'm grateful for that.

# Center of the Herd

Many of us have lived our lives without a feeling of connection. I suspect it is a problem with the head—full of information, prejudices, fear, judgment, and learned behavior that keeps us from feeling fully and openly with the heart. And safety, too, as though the heart is fragile and easily broken. And for some of us, it seems that way.

I now put myself, as much as I can, in healing experiences. This helps me let go, one by one, of old judgmental ideas. I work to see us all as being equal, whether we know it and act like it or not. I'm far from perfect at this practice, but I know it is the right path for me. I've come a long way, and I have a long way to go.

There have been several sources and tools to guide me on this path. One is my close affiliation with a twelve-step program, where I have stayed in the "center of the herd" for forty-plus years. Another resource that guides me, especially in my imperfection, is the prayer of St. Francis, known also for his trust and loving relationships with animals.

He wrote:

> Lord, make me an instrument of thy peace.
> That where there is hatred, I may bring love.
> That where there is wrong, I may bring the spirit of forgiveness.
> That where there is discord, I may bring harmony.
> That where there is error, I may bring truth.
> That where there is doubt, I may bring faith.
> That where there is despair, I may bring hope.
> That where there are shadows, I may bring light.
> That where there is sadness, I may bring joy.
> Lord, grant that I may seek rather to comfort than to be comforted.
> To understand, than to be understood
> To love, than to be loved.
> For it is by self-forgetting that one finds.
> It is by forgiving that one is forgiven.
> It is by dying that one awakens to Eternal Life.
> Amen.

*—St. Francis of Assisi*

# Outlaw?

I've often thought of myself as an outlaw. Not because I break laws, per se, but because I don't adhere to the unwritten social laws or codes.

Blame my family; we were brought up that way. We had a code of ethics different than the norm. We, all of us, never did anything just because others were doing it—we held ourselves to our high standards.

This often put us or me at odds with society. Superficial endeavors or conversations were OUT. We reached deep into our knowledge and experience of life and spoke from there—often startling those around us.

It's the right path for me. I enjoy the way it feels to be honest, to tell the truth, and to try to do it gently, but firmly.

# My Most Important Teacher
## How I Came to Emulate Admirable Behaviors

At this time in my life, between sixty and eighty years, I spend time with my primary teacher every day. I met her twelve years ago, an unexpected surprise, and although I was resistant to making the kind of commitment that would be required, especially financially, I said yes. During these years, and continuing every day, I have been presented with access to eight concepts which would make for a good life, but with which I had little familiarity.

1. End every encounter on a positive note
2. Lead with the Heart
3. Patience, Patience
4. If it isn't working after three tries, do it differently
5. Always be authentic, be your best self
6. Be completely present, wherever you are
7. It's not about power, but clear, honest communication
8. Ignore all of the above and you can easily get hurt

I can emulate her admirable behavior by being wholly present with her and staying open to learning what she has to teach. I need to become better and better in my part of the relationship; she's already a natural at her part. Rarely has she become angry with me, but when that has happened, I have made a real mistake. I don't let myself become distracted by talking; rather I stay tuned up and pay as close attention as I can. She's quick to forgive.

Trust has developed slowly, from the very start. I can see that she, too, has had experiences of betrayal. She calls out to me when she sees me coming, or hears my car approaching, but once I get there, she's quiet and seems content as we proceed.

She's a big girl and I could easily get hurt, but she would never do so intentionally. If something were to happen, it would be either carelessness on my part or not paying attention to, and honoring, her true nature.

Her name is Dakota, she weighs 1,100 pounds, and is my Draft-mix/Warmblood mare.

*Dakota and Kit*

Thank You

# Thank You

Cindy Tucker, Supervisor from
Sonoma County Office of Education:
my first boss at SCOE, she loved and supported
the detention library.

Aron Fogerson, Supervisor from Sonoma County
Main Adult Detention Facility:
my first jail boss; he respected, supported and
encouraged the detention library services.

Mates of the Main Adult Detention Facility and the
North County Detention Facility,
who were my inspiration.

Bonnie MacDonald, friend, who encouraged
this project since the writing began.

My family, who raised me in a way that built character.

Joelle Fraser, Non-Fiction Chief at the Mendocino Coast
Writer's Conference that year, whose praise
and editing of the jail writing nurtured publication.

Thursday, 1:30 memoir group at Wright Road,
for marvelous encouragement and feedback.

Skye Blaine and Berkana Publications for taking care
through the publication process.

Made in the USA
Las Vegas, NV
22 January 2021